What's So Spiritual About Your Gifts?

what's so spiritual about your gifts

LIFECHANGE BOOKS

Henry & Mel
BLACKABY

Multnomah Books

WHAT'S SO SPIRITUAL ABOUT YOUR GIFTS?

Published in association with the literary agency of Wolgemuth & Associates, Inc.

© 2004 by Henry T. Blackaby and Melvin Blackaby
International Standard Book Number: 978-1-59052-344-5

Cover image by Paul Taylor/Workbookstock

Unless otherwise indicated, Scripture quotations are from:
The Holy Bible, New King James Version © 1990 by Thomas Nelson, Inc.
Other Scripture quotations are from:
The Amplified Bible (AMP) © 1965, 1987 by Zondervan Publishing House.
New American Standard Bible® (NASB) © 1960, 1977, 1995
by the Lockman Foundation. Used by permission.

Italics in Scripture quotations are the authors' emphasis.

Published in the United States by Multnomah, an imprint of the Crown Publishing Group,
a division of Penguin Random House LLC, New York.

MULTNOMAH® and its mountain colophon are registered
trademarks of Penguin Random House LLC.

Printed in the United States of America

Library of Congress Cataloging-in-Publication Data

Blackaby, Henry T., 1935-
  What's so spiritual about your gifts? / by Henry Blackaby and Mel Blackaby.
     p. cm.
  ISBN 1-59052-344-X (hardcover)
  1. Holy Spirit. 2. Christian life.   I. Blackaby, Melvin D. II. Title.

  BT121.3.B55 2004
  234'.13--dc22

                              2003026158

                    17 — 11

Written for those who sincerely want to do the will of
God and experience the fullness of
His great salvation.
Jesus stood and cried out, saying,
"If anyone thirsts, let him come to Me and drink. He who
believes in Me, as the Scripture has said, out of his heart
will flow rivers of living water." But this He spoke
concerning the Spirit, whom those believing
in Him would receive...

JOHN 7:37B-39A

We dedicate this book
to the staff, leadership, and countless number of
servants with whom we have ministered.
Together we have seen
the Spirit of God move in power,
and it has been a privilege to serve the Lord with you.
Henry & Mel Blackaby

contents

THAT THE WORLD
MAY MARVEL

Looking back to the first century, it's easy to be amazed at the impact and accomplishments of the early believers in launching and multiplying the church. For such a monumental task, they seemed to possess such inadequate resources—no seminaries, no beautiful church facilities or sound systems or multimedia tools, no such thing as a Bible in every member's hand. They had no celebrities to endorse their cause, and very little freedom to promote their belief in Jesus Christ.

They were plain men and women for the most part,

insignificant and unknown, fighting against fierce opposition and hatred. But Scripture testifies that they "turned the world upside down"! (Acts 17:6). Wave after wave of persecution broke over them, yet they emerged victorious.

The message of the early church, as told in the book of Acts, is that the bare simplicity of the Christian faith is what counts. The testimony of these early Christians was that of God's people proclaiming the gospel in the power of the Holy Spirit…and confirming it with holy lives.

So what's their secret?

A GIFT RELEASED, A WORLD AMAZED

There is no secret. The Bible openly tells us of a gift from God that unleashes the power and wisdom of His kingdom, providing everything we need for life and godliness (2 Peter 1:3). Just before Jesus ascended into heaven, He instructed the apostles to "wait for the Promise of the Father," which He explained in these words: "You shall be baptized with the Holy Spirit not many days from now…. You shall receive power when the Holy Spirit has come upon you; and you shall be witnesses to Me…" (Acts 1:4–5, 8).

The result of the Holy Spirit coming upon the disciples was something earthshaking. No, it extended much further than that—these Spirit-filled believers literally shook the gates of hell. So dramatic was the Spirit's coming upon them that onlookers could not help but be in awe: "They were all amazed and marveled"; "they were all amazed and perplexed"; "they were filled with wonder and amazement"; "they marveled" (Acts 2:7, 12; 3:10; 4:13).

Does the world marvel at the church today?

Unfortunately, much of what happens in the contemporary church is little more than a reflection of the values and the reasoning of the surrounding culture, instead of a clear demonstration of God's power. Why is this?

CATCH THE ASSIGNMENT...AND THE THRILL

For most Christians, when it comes to discovering our part in the work of God's kingdom, the question we ask is self-centered: "What can I do for God?" The question we should be asking is God-centered: "What does God want to do through me? What is His particular assignment *for me?*" To make that subtle shift in thinking—

and to experience the true giftedness of the Holy Spirit that follows from it—will have dramatic results in your life, for what you'll witness will be God's power to transform lives, not just your own ability to help people in need.

This book is not an exhaustive study on the Holy Spirit, but it will reorient your thinking to biblical teaching on the Spirit's role in your life, clarify the apparent confusion between natural talents and spiritual gifts, and help you get in step with God's purpose. It will guide you practically as you seek to better understand the Spirit's assignment and to experience God's great salvation in every area of your life.

And as you understand more about the strategic plan in God's heart for sending the gift of the Holy Spirit, you won't struggle with burnout serving God or carry the weight of anxiety and stress. Your Christian life will produce joy, and you'll discover that merely watching the activity of God from a distance could never compare with the thrill of being fully involved in the Spirit's active work.

FIRST—THE RELATIONSHIP

Why is it that countless believers seem to stand powerless before a world desperately needing what we claim to have? Why does the church have so little impact? Why are so many Christians so frustrated?

There are probably several reasons, but a major one is that Christians are seeking *gifts* of the Holy Spirit and not the Holy Spirit Himself. They want power but not a relationship with the One whose presence gives power. They want to do great things for God, but haven't understood that greatness in the kingdom of God comes out of a relationship with Christ and the filling of the Holy Spirit. They're so enamored with self that they have no idea what is on the heart of God.

If we seek the gifts of the Spirit and not the Holy Spirit Himself, we'll always focus on self. We must learn to understand that *there are no gifts* apart from an intimate relationship with the Spirit.

How fully do you appreciate what this relationship means?

WHAT'S NEW WITH YOU?

For the Christian, faith is not asking for what we don't have, but making use of what God says we already possess. It's simply trusting God's Word to be true. Nowhere else is this more profoundly true than in what is given us in God's Spirit.

The Bible says every Christian is "a new creation; old things have passed away; behold, all things have become new" (2 Corinthians 5:17). So what's new?

Mainly this: You've been forgiven of sin, cleansed of all unrighteousness, clothed in the righteousness of Christ…and given the gift of the Holy Spirit to dwell within you. To be a Christian is to have a new spiritual life, a new relationship with God, a new authority in heaven and on earth, and a new power to serve. All this comes as we receive the gift of the Holy Spirit.

This spiritual transformation deep within a person is the heart of God's great salvation. Christians are not mere mortals, but born-again citizens of the kingdom of God who live in a spiritual realm that the unbelieving world cannot understand. So if there's little difference between one who claims to be a Christian and the unbelieving world…something is desperately wrong.

BETTER THAN JESUS AT OUR SIDE

One of the most overlooked verses in the Bible is John 16:7. Jesus said, "I tell you the truth. It is to your advantage that I go away; for if I do not go away, the Helper [the Holy Spirit] will not come to you; but if I depart, I will send Him to you." What an amazing statement! Jesus told His disciples they would be better off if He left and the Spirit came. Better to have the Holy Spirit within you than Jesus beside you.

But that's hard to believe. What could possibly be better than having Jesus Christ physically present?

Peter was one who couldn't comprehend what Jesus

was saying that night in the upper room. Peter had always fought hard to keep Him close, even rebuking Jesus when He talked of going to the cross. On the Mount of Transfiguration, it was Peter who had wanted to build a permanent structure and stay there. Later, when soldiers came to Gethsemane to arrest Jesus, it was Peter who drew his sword and cut off the ear of one of those who was trying to take Him away.

It wasn't long, however, before Peter understood what Jesus meant that night. Pentecost came and the promise of the coming Spirit was fulfilled. Peter and the other disciples were filled with the Holy Spirit, never again to be the same. Peter, who had been self-pleasing, self-trusting, and self-seeking, had now died to self. Peter, who was full of sin, continually getting into trouble, foolish and impetuous, had now been filled with the Spirit. And the mighty power of God flowed in and through his life.

"Many want the Spirit's power but not the Spirit's purity. The Holy Spirit does not rent out His attributes. His power is never separated from His glorious Self."

—JAMES A. STEWART

Heaven's Throne Gift

FOR EACH AND ALL

The empowerment that Peter experienced is for every believer, not just those who are "called into the ministry." The fullness of the Spirit is not reserved for the spiritual giant or the supersaint whom God deems qualified. No, the Spirit is given to sinners and failures who have learned to repent and have come to realize the cleansing blood of Jesus over their lives. The Spirit is given to those who recognize their need and cry out for God's help.

Everyone who believes God's good news of salvation and commits his life to Jesus Christ will receive the same Holy Spirit who indwelt the Son of God. The power demonstrated in His life—and in His resurrection from the dead—was the power of the Holy Spirit working within Him.

The same is true for all believers. Paul said, "If the Spirit of Him who raised Jesus from the dead dwells in you, He who raised Christ from the dead will also give life to your mortal bodies through His Spirit who dwells in you" (Romans 8:11).

That's what we need to hear today! Resurrection power is found in the Holy Spirit, the Holy Spirit is found in every believer, and the measure in which we walk in the Spirit's fullness and power is the measure in which our lives will impact the world around us. "'Not by might nor by power, but by My Spirit,' says the LORD of hosts" (Zechariah 4:6).

NO WALK, NO GIFT

We've often heard people confess to being far from the Lord—while in the next breath they tell us what their "spiritual gift" is! Such a disconnect between the Spirit and His gifts is impossible.

We must understand a simple principle: *If you do not walk in the Spirit, you do not have a spiritual gift.* Apart from the Spirit, whatever "gifts" we display can only be our natural talents, drawing attention to self.

Believers often ask each other (or themselves), "What's your spiritual gift?" The true answer to that question is this: The *Holy Spirit* is the gift. He Himself is the indispensable gift of God to your life. He's the third person of the Trinity, just as needful in your life as the other two.

This singular gift of the Spirit is God's full provision for our life. In the Spirit, the Lord has given us everything we need: He's the open door to heaven's wisdom. He's our source of power for every assignment. His presence within us is the crowning work of God's great salvation toward those who believe—*for the glory of God.*

"I used to ask God to help me. Then I asked if I might help Him. I ended up by asking Him to do His work through me."

–HUDSON TAYLOR

Hudson Taylor's Spiritual Secret

Spiritual gifts are bestowed on believers according to the purposes of God and distributed by the sovereign wisdom of God. Our spiritual gifts never belong to us; they're an expression of the Holy Spirit doing the Father's will.

Never forget that the Spirit is given to each one to equip us to do God's will, not our will. Paul said that "one and the same Spirit works all these things, distributing to each one individually *as He wills*" (1 Corinthians 12:11). You cannot convince the Holy Spirit to do what He doesn't want to do, and He *always* wants to do the Father's will. In other words, if you're living outside His will, it's impossible to function according to any "spiritual gift" you may think you have, for you aren't walking in the Spirit. The Spirit manifests Himself in our lives to accomplish God's purpose and bring glory to God.

GOD'S PURPOSE FOR THE GIFT

We learn much about God's purpose in giving the Holy Spirit when we ponder the profound statement Paul made in 1 Corinthians 12:7: "The manifestation of the Spirit is given to each one for the profit of all." Each phrase in that verse is important; each must be applied to your life.

"The manifestation of the Spirit" means the Spirit will reveal *Himself* and His activity in you. Are you ready for Him to do it? Are you expecting Him to do His work? Be assured that He is ready to accomplish the Father's purposes in your life.

Paul also said that the Holy Spirit would manifest himself "to each one." That means nobody is overlooked. *You* have received the gift of the Holy Spirit, and He will manifest Himself in *your* life.

We hear people complaining about the talents and skills they lack, then concluding, "I don't have anything to offer God." That's likely true, but what does that have to do with the Holy Spirit working in your life? When He's present, it doesn't matter what *you* can or cannot do. If you don't have a lot of natural talent, you can thank God that you're the perfect vessel for Him to show Himself powerful in you. Listen to His promise: "My grace is sufficient for you, for My strength is made perfect in weakness" (2 Corinthians 12:9). In your weakness, He is strong. *You* are the person in whom He can do His best work, for He will get all the glory.

The final part of Paul's statement about the Spirit in 1 Corinthians 12:7 is especially crucial: "for the profit of all." There's a corporate dimension to everything God does in your life. Every gift He has given is to be shared within the life of His people. If we aren't actively building up the body, we aren't functioning as God desires. The Holy Spirit will always seek to build the unity of the body, a unity that is precious in the heart of God.

Hear it once more: The Holy Spirit Himself is God's gift to you. The same Holy Spirit who manifested Himself in the life of Jesus and in the early believers has been sent to work through you. If you open your life to Him, He will manifest His power in your life.

WHAT THE SPIRIT IS SAYING...

If the Holy Spirit at this time is impressing truth upon your spirit, you must respond immediately. This moment will not merely *lead* you to an encounter with God; this moment *is* an encounter with God.

So what is God's Spirit saying to you? Are you seeking on your own to do good things for God, or do you allow Him to do His will through you? Do you need to make major adjustments in how you relate to the Holy Spirit?

Take a moment with the Lord in prayer...

*Heavenly Father, I realize that I've neglected
the person of the Holy Spirit in my life.
I repent, asking You to forgive me for relegating
Him to a position much less than He deserves.
May I know and experience the gift
of the Holy Spirit in all His fullness.
I open my life for Him to teach me, lead me,
and work through me. Amen.*

chapter two

THE TALENT
TRAP

Anchor this truth in your mind: The gift of the Holy Spirit is primarily about God and His work, not about you and your work.

Most of the discussions we hear today about spiritual gifts revolve around what people are good at doing or what people most like to do. That approach tends to be self-glorifying: If we operate only according to our talents and ability, we get the glory. But if we function according to the power of the Spirit, God gets the glory as others around us see Him at work. And God's goal is to reveal *Himself* to a watching world—not to showcase our achievements.

YOUR BEST–OR GOD'S?

In equipping us to do God's will, the Holy Spirit doesn't give us a talent, skill, or ability to use as we desire; He gives us Himself, then *He* accomplishes the Father's will through our lives. This alone makes possible our experience of the divine power that turns the world upside down.

Yet too often we're content to serve God by giving our own greatest effort. What is that, however, compared to the power of the Holy Spirit? What does the world really need—to see what we can do or what God can do?

How strange it must sound to God when we counsel others (or ourselves), "Just do your best, that's all that matters." Do we want to give the world our best, or let the world experience God's best? To give them only the best we have is to cheat the world of what could have been.

Living by the Spirit's power doesn't mean we should ignore our God-given abilities and talents. But never assume those talents are the only areas in which you can serve. We'll say more later about how we use our natural talents, but we need to first expose the myth that our natural talents are the same as spiritual gifts. They may, in fact, be worlds apart.

MISSING OUT ON SEEING GOD

When it comes to serving God, we tend to evaluate what we're good at and what we like to do, then serve according to our ability. We figure out what talents we have, then offer them to God, assuming that these are our spiritual gifts.

This, in fact, is what others usually encourage us to do—to recognize where we're proficient and what we like to do, then serve according to our ability, all the while asking God to bless our efforts. We never consider serving outside the areas of our strength, and can't imagine God asking us to do that which we don't like to do. We look at ourselves to discover our assignment from God.

The result: We don't need or rely on the Holy Spirit because we're confident in our abilities and are under the delusion that we have everything under control. The world, therefore, looks at the church and sees good people doing good things for God, but they don't see the power of God working through His people to accomplish *what only He could do.*

WHAT'S HARD FOR THE RICHLY TALENTED

Among many startling statements Jesus made to people of His day was this one: "It is easier for a camel to go through the eye of a needle than for a rich man to enter the kingdom of God" (Matthew 19:24). This was an astounding assertion that went against everything the people had been taught. They'd always assumed wealth was a sign of God's blessing, but Jesus knew that wealth causes people to feel self-sufficient and can lead them away from God. Rich people may never know how to walk by faith and to experience the provision of God, for they already have everything they need and rely on their own abilities to obtain what they want.

The same is true with those who are blessed with many natural talents. It's easier for a camel to go through a needle's eye than for a man with great talents to be used in the kingdom of God, for that person will be tempted to rely on his or her ability rather than the power of the Holy Spirit. He or she may even begin to confuse the natural abilities they possess with God's enabling Holy Spirit. And once a person's talents become a substitute for the work of the Holy Spirit, that person is of no use to God.

———————————— ✺ ————————————

"Among the variety of God's gifts, some are natural abilities and character qualities sanctified, while others correspond to nothing that was previously seen in the person's life."

– J. I. PACKER

Experiencing God's Presence

THE DANGER OF SPIRITUAL INVENTORIES

One of the ways we're sometimes tempted to operate according to natural talents instead of by the Spirit is through various tests known as "spiritual gift inventories." These tests have become popular, but they can be confusing for many, because of their inherent limitations. If a non-Christian took such a test, then took it again a few months later after becoming a Christian, it would probably produce the exact same results. Yet why should we now call something a "spiritual gift" when it would be viewed as nothing more than a "natural talent" only months earlier?

Taking a spiritual gift inventory test can help you understand where you're strong and where you're weak. It can even help identify how God has used you since you've become a Christian. But it shouldn't be used as a guide for how God desires to use you in the future, for God's purposes are based upon His strengths, not yours alone. He may choose to take you into areas of service in which you're naturally weak, to reveal His strength and bring glory to Himself.

One of the dangers of relying on a spiritual gift inventory test is that you'll be tempted to trust the test results and not turn to God. You may lock in your "gifts" and identify your field of service, and therefore not be free to follow Christ in a new assignment. Our service to God should not be a result of a written test, but should flow from a dynamic relationship with our living Lord whereby He guides our life day by day.

BETTER THAN KNOWING YOURSELF

So what about our natural talents and past experience? Will God use them, or will He always use our lives in areas we're naturally weak?

God created you with your unique abilities, and He *does* want to use them. But He's far more interested in you knowing Him than He is you knowing your abilities. The world tells us to affirm self, but God tells us to deny self. Your identity and self-worth aren't found in your abilities, but in your relationship to Christ.

The reason we're often sidetracked on this point is that it's *so much easier* to simply do what you're good at than it is to walk with God and obey Him when He asks us to do what we're unable to do in our own strength. That kind of obedience requires a relationship where we know His will, a faith that trusts His will, and a humble spirit that submits to His will.

When we do obey, however, God can accomplish more in six days than we could do in sixty years with our best efforts alone. In fact, without the Spirit working through our lives, everything we do is dead works. Jesus wasn't exaggerating when He said, "I am the vine, you are the branches. He who abides in Me, and I in him, bears much fruit; for *without Me you can do nothing*" (John 15:5). We rarely consider that God gave us His Spirit because "self" could never accomplish the assignment He has for us. Only through His Spirit are we equipped for service.

DO THE IMPOSSIBLE?

So the question to ask is this: Will God ever ask you to do something you aren't able to do?

Yes, all the time! God wants to use your life in a whole new world of opportunity beyond your areas of competence and experience.

So never put limits on how God can use your life. Obey almighty God and trust that He knows what He's doing in your life. Don't look at your abilities and natural talents alone and serve only in the areas you feel competent. If you do, you'll eliminate yourself from significant arenas of service.

We are servants, and Christ is our Master. The servant never tells the Master what he or she wants to do for Him. The servant simply obeys the Master. Could you imagine the Master giving an order to the servant and the servant replying, "Sorry, that isn't my gift"?

So we must learn to seek God's will and obey Him no matter how difficult and uncomfortable the assignment and no matter how high the cost—knowing that we're called to accomplish those tasks not according to our own capacity, but according to the fully enabling power of the Holy Spirit.

THE PATTERN IN JESUS

Have you noticed that the gospel writers never mention any of Jesus' physical attributes or special talents? Instead, they continually point to the work of the Holy Spirit in His life.

We see this first in a big way at the time of Jesus' baptism. Something spectacular happened there at the Jordan River, something that initiated a new role for the Spirit in His life: "When all the people were baptized, it came to pass that Jesus also was baptized; and while He prayed, the heaven was opened. And the Holy Spirit descended in bodily form like a dove upon Him, and a voice came from heaven which said, 'You are My beloved Son; in You I am well pleased.'" (Luke 3:21–22). This moment represented the beginning of a new stage in Jesus' life, a special anointing by the Father for extraordinary and demanding tasks.

From the moment Jesus began His public ministry, the work of the Holy Spirit enabled Him to do everything the Father asked of Him. The Scriptures make this clear. Immediately after Jesus' baptism, Luke tells us that "Jesus, *being filled with the Holy Spirit*, returned from the Jordan and was led by the Spirit into the wilderness"

(Luke 4:1). Immediately after being tempted in the wilderness by the devil, "Jesus returned in the *power of the Spirit* to Galilee, and news of Him went out through all the surrounding region" (Luke 4:14).

Jesus went to Nazareth, where we see Him speak with clarity of the assignment God had given Him. Standing in the synagogue, He turned in the Scriptures to Isaiah and read, "*The Spirit of the LORD is upon Me,* because He has anointed Me to preach the gospel to the poor; He has sent Me to heal the brokenhearted, to proclaim liberty to the captives and recovery of sight to the blind, to set at liberty those who are oppressed; to proclaim the acceptable year of the LORD." Jesus then added, "Today this Scripture is fulfilled in your hearing" (Luke 4:18–21).

So we see the pattern: The assignment was given by the Father, accepted by the Son, and fulfilled through the working power of the Spirit.

JESUS THE MAN

Jesus fulfilled His assignment as a man filled with the Holy Spirit, a man in whom the Holy Spirit was empowering His every move. It's clear He chose continually to yield His life to the Holy Spirit that the Father might do His work through Him. "My food is to do the will of Him who sent Me," He told the people, "and to finish His work" (John 4:34).

He suggested the limitations of His ability when He said, "The Son can do nothing of Himself, but what He sees the Father do" (John 5:19). To those who questioned where He received His wisdom, He answered, "My doctrine is not Mine, but His who sent Me. If anyone wants to do His will, he shall know concerning the doctrine, whether it is from God or whether I speak on My own authority" (John 7:16–17). He said to others, "I do nothing of Myself; but as My Father taught Me, I speak these things. And He who sent Me is with Me. The Father has not left Me alone, for I always do those things that please Him" (John 8:28–29).

Likewise Jesus told His disciples in the upper room, "The words that I speak to you I do not speak on My own authority; but the Father who dwells in Me does the works" (John 14:10).

Never overlook the source of Jesus' power while He walked on earth in the flesh. We tend to excuse His miracles by saying, "It was easy for Him, He was God!" But when the Son of God chose to come and dwell among us, He laid aside that which was rightfully His and lived like a man. "Although He existed in the form of God," Jesus "did not regard equality with God a thing to be grasped, but emptied Himself, taking the form of a bond-servant, and being made in the likeness of men" (Philippians 2:6–7, NASB).

Jesus chose to live with all the limitations of a human being. Why? Because He could not take our place unless He first took up our condition. Salvation was dependent upon a *man* named Jesus dying on the cross for our sins. His life is therefore a demonstration of the way in which we *can* live, full of the Holy Spirit.

ALWAYS IN THE SPIRIT

Even the teaching that Jesus gave the disciples after He had risen from the dead was accomplished through the Spirit. Luke tells us that Jesus ascended into heaven "after He *through the Holy Spirit* had given commandments to the apostles whom He had chosen" (Acts 1:2). And the final commandment Jesus gave them was to wait themselves for the coming of the Holy Spirit upon their lives. He knew they couldn't do the Father's will without the Spirit; but *in* the Spirit all things were possible.

And so it happened. Once the Spirit had come upon them, the apostles began doing everything the people had seen Jesus do. They healed the sick, raised the dead, and taught with great authority and power—and lives were changed.

And it can happen that way in our lives and ministry as well.

WHAT THE SPIRIT IS SAYING...

You may be one who loves the Lord with all your heart, but never knew what to do about it. You've worked hard and tried your best. But you have yet to experience *His* best working through you. Is that what you want? Have you been living according to your natural ability without considering what the Holy Spirit was doing in your life? Have your abilities even kept you from seeking Him with all your heart? You may want to stop for a prayer of response to what you've heard.

Heavenly Father, forgive me for giving others my best
when You wanted them to know You.
Enable me to release my life to the work of the Holy Spirit,
that You may be glorified in me.
Show me Your will that I may adjust
my plans to Your activity. Amen.

chapter three

THOSE WHOM GOD USES

Here's a typical scenario in our churches: The right person is being sought to serve as chairman of the finance committee, and the church turns immediately to someone such as a banker or businessman who has been very successful, financially speaking. However, the church gives no thought to whether that person has even the faintest idea of how to walk by faith and trust in God. He or she then steps into the position and by all appearances manages the church's money well—so well that the church never experiences what God could have done if they had trusted more in Him.

It seems as though our tendency is always to judge a person's usefulness to God in terms of external factors. But the fact is, those whom everyone expects to succeed because of their apparent strengths or their great and numerous talents are more often the ones most likely to fail in the work of the kingdom of God. They're especially in danger if they listen to the press reports on how good they are.

God, however, in choosing and calling His servants, focuses not on outward appearances but on their heart and their walk with Him.

(from Henry) A FATHER'S LEGACY

My father was a branch manager for a bank all my life. Fortunately, he was a Christian businessman with great spiritual integrity. He was one of the godliest men I've ever known. Contrary to many of his colleagues, he knew God and walked by faith. He helped finance small businesses not by the world's standards but by God's. He based his choices on character and potential good, often to the amazement of others. And God blessed not only his work at the bank but also the entire community.

I recall that he would often talk about the danger of "choosing leaders" based on natural skill rather than on spiritual integrity and maturity. He was very concerned about people and their impact upon God's work.

Now I want you to know that God is using men and women of great talent and ability. But when He does, the first assignment of the Holy Spirit is to bring humility. They must cease to compare themselves to others and measure themselves against Almighty God. The Holy Spirit must deal with their self-image and replace it with the image of Christ. That is not an easy task.

But hear the word of the Lord: "On this one will I look: on him who is poor and of a contrite spirit, and who trembles at My word" (Isaiah 66:2). Therein is the key for every person who is used of God, a humble estimation of self and a reverent esteem for God. His eyes are upon those who have a deep hunger for the Bible; for they know it leads to the way of life.

WHERE GOD LOOKS

Be assured that when God determines whether to use you in His work, He isn't on the lookout for someone talented, good-looking, well spoken of, and highly educated. He's searching above all for one whose heart is pure. When He finds someone pure in heart, He'll fill that heart with His Spirit and move through that person's life with power. "For the eyes of the LORD run to and fro throughout the whole earth, to show Himself strong on behalf of those whose heart is loyal ["blameless"— *Amplified Bible*] to Him" (2 Chronicles 16:9).

This promise is given to every believer, for we all have the capacity to choose the master to whom we give our heart. We've been "set free from sin" through Jesus Christ and are now "slaves of righteousness" (Romans 6:18).

Paul reminded the Corinthians of how God works:

For you see your calling, brethren, that not many wise according to the flesh, not many mighty, not many noble, are called. But God has chosen the foolish things of the world to put to shame the wise, and God has chosen the weak things of the world to put to shame the things which are mighty; and the base things of the world and the things which are despised God has chosen, and the things which are not, to bring to nothing the things that are, that no flesh should glory in His presence.

1 CORINTHIANS 1:26–29

Paul could even point to his own life in this regard, knowing he was "the least of the apostles" and unworthy to even be an apostle because of past persecution of Christians (1 Corinthians 15:9); yet God was gracious to use Paul mightily.

When God has a task that needs a laborer, He doesn't go looking for one who has the right gifts. He looks for one who has an obedient heart, so He can accomplish the task through that person and receive all the glory.

———————— ✑ ————————

"The Spirit's fullness is not the reward of our faithfulness, but God's gift for our defeat.
He was not given to the disciples in Acts 28 as the culmination and reward of their wonderful service, but in Acts 2 when they had proved themselves cowards, meeting behind barred doors."

– ROY HESSION

Be Filled Now

Remember the Lord's words to the prophet Samuel after sending him to find and anoint Israel's king? God said, "For the LORD does not see as man sees; for man looks at the outward appearance, but the LORD looks at the heart" (1 Samuel 16:7). Have you been looking at your "outward appearance" and your "physical attributes" as a gauge for your service to God? That isn't what the Lord is looking at. The Lord looks at your heart. What is the condition of your heart?

ALL SO ORDINARY

There are many examples in the Bible of God using people who had no ability of their own to accomplish His purposes. Take Gideon for example. He was probably the last person anyone would have chosen to lead God's people into battle. God, however, saw him as a "mighty man of valor" (Judges 6:12)—even though when the angel of the Lord came to him, Gideon was hiding from the enemy and threshing wheat in a winepress for fear they would steal his food.

When the Lord gave him an assignment, Gideon's response was honest: "O my Lord, how can I save Israel? Indeed my clan is the weakest in Manasseh, and I am the least in my father's house" (v. 15). Gideon was right; he had no abilities that would enable him to lead the people into battle. "But the Spirit of the LORD came upon

Gideon" (Judges 6:34), and God's power was displayed through him and his men.

The result of Gideon's obedience: With three hundred men he defeated an army of 120,000. Impossible? For Gideon, yes, but not for God! Therefore the watching world gave glory to God, for only He could have given such a victory.

Consider also the prophet Amos. His book of prophecy in the Bible begins, "The words of Amos, who was among the sheepbreeders of Tekoa." Amos was a nobody from an insignificant place. He cared for sheep and (as we discover later) worked as a migrant laborer in fruit orchards. What in his background qualified him to stand before the king and boldly pronounce God's word? Nothing. Yet he was greatly used of God for a special assignment as the Spirit enabled him.

Peter was only a fisherman, unpolished, rough, abrasive, and speaking the tongue of a commoner. Could he lead the disciples, preach the first gospel sermon at Pentecost, stand in the temple courts defying the religious elite, and write words that would go down in Scripture? Wrong question! The right question is this: Can the Holy Spirit work through an ordinary laborer named Peter? Yes! A thousand times yes!

GOD'S MAKEOVER

Think again about those men and what God did through them. Then consider this: If Gideon had taken a spiritual gift inventory to determine his future course of action, his chances for taking a job as a military general would be almost nil.

If they'd had their spiritual gifts analyzed, Amos wouldn't have stood before the king and Peter wouldn't have become an apostle. David would never have been king of Israel, Joseph would not have ruled in Egypt, Nehemiah wouldn't have rebuilt the walls of Jerusalem, and Paul wouldn't have been a missionary.

If pursuing God's work depended on their own perceived abilities, most if not all of our heroes of the faith would have never become known. After evaluating their strengths and abilities, they most likely would have concluded they didn't have what it takes to meet the awesome task before them. The assignment just didn't match their "gift set."

Today we see these people as champions of the faith, but that's only because we've seen the last chapter of their lives. If you'd met them before their encounter with the Lord and their filling by the Spirit, you would find them to be very unassuming people, as ordinary as you and me, and often poor, weak, and insignificant.

Makeovers are currently popular among TV shows, and seeing the before and after is often dramatic. But no Hollywood makeover can compare to the work of the Holy Spirit to transform a person's life. His specialty is using ordinary men and women in extraordinary ways.

(from Mel) NOT LOOKING THE PART

I had to laugh when our church went through the process of electing new deacons. The church had made their nominations, I and the chairman were interviewing the candidates, and one particular man made a fascinating comment. With a look of bewilderment he said, "But I don't *look* like a deacon!"

In his mind he saw a picture of someone in a nice suit, theologically educated, straitlaced and clean-cut. This man, however, served in the police force, raced cars professionally, and didn't wear suits. In his mind, he didn't have the right gifts, but the church recognized that he had the right heart. He was a man of character. And the Lord can equip a man like that to do whatever the assignment requires of him. This man soon recognized God's call, accepted the assignment, and has been used of God to bless the church.

WHAT THE SPIRIT IS SAYING...

Do you sense that God wants to use your life, but you thought you had nothing to offer Him? Don't merely look at what you have to offer the world; seek the heart of God and allow His Spirit to work through you. He'll touch the world in ways you could never touch it on your own. Perhaps the Holy Spirit has just invited you to a greater task in the work of God's kingdom. Take a moment to respond in prayer.

Heavenly Father, I never thought I had much
to offer You, but I was wrong.
You don't want my talents alone;
You want me to trust and obey You.
I've been more concerned with the things I want to do for
You than the things You want to do through me.
More concerned about the talents I don't possess
than the gift of the Spirit I do possess.
Forgive me for relying on myself,
and help me to trust You more. Amen.

chapter four

GIFTING FOLLOWS ASSIGNMENT

God sent the Holy Spirit on assignment. The question we must therefore ask is this: In each of our lives, what is that assignment? Why was the Spirit sent to you, and what is He doing in your life? How do you get in step with Him and enjoy abundant life as Christ has promised?

As the Spirit reveals the will of the Father, we can then allow Him to accomplish it through our lives by the Spirit's enabling. *Equipping always follows the assignment.* The enabling power of the Holy Spirit *follows* the assignment, never precedes it. For if we aren't willing to obey the Lord and do His will, there's no need for Him to give us gifts.

Spiritual gifts don't belong to the believer; they're an expression of the Holy Spirit doing the Father's will.

(from Mel) GOD AT WORK

I was twenty-one years old, driving east across the Mojave Desert in 115-degree weather—in a car with black vinyl interior, no air-conditioning, and an engine that was overheating. I was in trouble.

In the distance I saw a dark cloud coming my way. My deliverance! The rain was sure to cool things down, giving much-needed relief. But to my surprise, it wasn't a rainstorm I ran into, but a sandstorm.

Overcome with dust, feeling faint from the scorching weather, and with a stressed-out car, I searched for a place to stop and find help. I was in the middle of nowhere, but eventually I came to a run-down gas station.

The only shade available was the building's shadow, so I pulled around back and parked the car. I got out, opened the hood, and began tinkering with the engine.

Suddenly I realized I was being watched. A drifter was standing about thirty feet away, just staring. His hair was unkempt and his face unshaven, and a scar went from his forehead, across his eyelid, and ended below his chin. I was nervous. No, I was downright scared!

As the man began to walk straight at me, many things went through my head. "I'm going to die; nobody will ever find my body; I want my mommy!" Knowing that I couldn't run and nobody was there to help, I decided the next best thing was to flash a big smile and hold out my hand to greet a new friend. As we began to talk, he made a fascinating statement. He said, "As I watched you work on your car, you radiated friendliness and I had to come and meet you."

Immediately I sensed in my spirit what was going on. The Lord was at work and I needed to respond. I quickly identified for the man what he saw—the Spirit of God dwelling in my life. As I expected, he was ripe for the picking and responded positively toward Christ.

What happened? The Father wanted to speak to a desperate man, and He happened to have one of His children driving by. Looking back, I know why my car was overheating, why the storm caused me to stop, and why I ended up behind an old gas station in the backside of the desert. God was at work around me...and the Holy Spirit within me was responding to the orders given by the Father.

IN THE MIDDLE OF GOD'S ACTIVITY

The divine nature cannot be hidden. It must, and it will, express itself.

When our lives are yielded to the Spirit's control, God is certain to work through us in leaving His mark on those around us. For He not only has given us new life, He has extended an invitation to be involved in His work to redeem this world. The Holy Spirit's major assignment is to bring our lives in harmony with God's activity so He can accomplish this work through us.

Have you understood His assignment in *your* life to bring you into the middle of God's activity? One way to begin approaching this is to review your past.

SPIRITUAL MARKERS

Never neglect what you have seen God do in your life. Take a careful look at these things from God's perspective, all the way from your birth to where you stand right now—it's all very significant. If you have special talents, use them in the Lord's service. Help another person in need if you have the ability to do so. Step up and bless your church by doing those things that others couldn't do. In other words, be a servant! Don't stand back and watch others struggle when you know you have the ability to lend a hand.

Acts of service, however, are different than the unique assignments God will lay upon your heart. We should always be ready to step up and serve the body of Christ, but what exactly has God called you to invest your life in? What are the ministries that have captured your heart? Is the Lord using your life in such a way that you know the pleasure of God? And what is it that requires the work of the Holy Spirit in order to accomplish the task?

"The commands of God are enablings.
God banks entirely on His own Spirit,
and when we attempt,
His ability is granted immediately.
We have a great deal more power than we know."
– OSWALD CHAMBERS
He Shall Glorify Me

As you seek to walk in the center of God's will, it's important to establish the spiritual markers in your life that have led you up to the place you now stand. Those moments when you knew God was working and chose to use your life. God doesn't work by accident or happenstance. Everything He does in your life will lead to the next step in your relationship to Him. Looking back on what God has done in your life may bring great clarity toward what He wants to do in your life in the days to come. So bring your past into the present, and ask God to direct your future.

RELATIONSHIP IS THE KEY

Here again we must emphasize this truth: *The relationship is the key.* You must know Christ well enough that you already know your answer before He tells you the assignment. The answer must be "Yes, Lord." You'll need to trust that God knows what He's doing.

We must never look first at ourselves, our abilities, and our desires to determine whether we'll obey or not. He is our Lord! And if we don't have a heart of obedience, He may choose not to show us His will. For if we knew His will and still chose not to obey, it would be far better not to have known at all. His mercy withholds the revelation of His will until we're ready to obey. For every time we choose not to obey His clear direction, there comes hardness in our heart. But when our heart is prepared to obey, the Holy Spirit has absolute freedom to lead us on the exciting adventure of following God.

Remember again that God is always looking upon the heart. If you're having a hard time hearing from God to know His assignment, perhaps He knows that your heart isn't ready to respond if He did speak. That's what God is waiting for, a heart that is surrendered and ready to obey before you ever hear Him speak.

Are you ready for God to reveal His assignment in your life? *Any* assignment? Are you prepared to say yes before you know what He'll ask? That may be the key to knowing and doing the will of God. Your heart must be convinced that He is God and He is Lord.

(from Henry) OBEYING IN EVERYTHING

I've always believed that a Christian is primarily called not to a vocation, but to a relationship. Our service comes out of our relationship to God through Jesus Christ, and anything He asks, I obey. Many are surprised when they discover all the areas of ministry I have served. I've been a youth leader, music minister, education minister, senior pastor, director of missions, president of a Bible college, director for prayer and spiritual awakening, conference speaker, and writer of many books. Is that because I'm multitalented?

No, it is only because I've sought to be obedient to the Master in all things, and the Holy Spirit has enabled me to serve when God assigns.

Nobody is more surprised at what God is doing through my life than I am. I know my limitations but have also come to know the unlimited resources of the Holy Spirit. Some have asked me if I have a life verse that has guided my life. I don't usually use those terms, but if I did the verse might be Daniel 3:17, "Our God whom we serve is able...and He will." The reason I've seen so many miracles in my life is that I've never doubted God's ability to work...and He has.

ASSIGNMENTS AND GIFTING FOR THE APOSTLES

Jesus wanted His followers to understand the difference between their best effort and the power of the Holy Spirit. So He sent out seventy disciples two by two into the harvest to prepare the way for Him to minister in the area. As He sent them, He gave them power and authority to fulfill the assignment.

Afterward they could hardly believe what they had seen God do through their lives. They ministered to people everywhere, healing the sick and proclaiming the kingdom of God. The Scripture says they "returned with joy, saying, 'Lord, even the demons are subject to us in Your name.' And He said to them, 'I saw Satan fall like lightning from heaven. Behold, I give you the authority....'" (Luke 10:17–19).

Jesus let them have a taste of what was to come. This power and authority was not a permanent gift; it was for *that* assignment. They didn't have natural ability to do what He needed done, so He gave it to them. As such, they got a foretaste of what was to come with the outpouring of the Holy Spirit on the day of Pentecost. They would come to know that anything was possible for God, and if He sent them He would also equip them.

(from Henry) GOD'S WORK, NOT OURS

Have you ever had one of those assignments from God that was overwhelming? That seems to be my life story.

But one particular assignment especially made me feel like a fish out of water.

I was informed that I would be speaking to the president and vice president in the Oval Office. In fact, I was told that I could talk with them about anything I wanted. As I prepared, I thought to myself, *What should I say to the president of the United States?* Immediately the Holy Spirit reminded me, "The Father has not given you this opportunity so you can tell the president what is on your heart. You are an ambassador of God, to share what's on *His* heart."

My line of thinking had to be adjusted from self to God. The Holy Spirit was there to enable me to fulfill the Father's purpose. This is not about us! What does God want to do with our lives? I was encouraged to read Luke 12:11–12, "Now when they bring you to the synagogues and magistrates and authorities, do not worry about how or what you should answer, or what you should say. For the Holy Spirit will teach you in that very hour what you ought to say." Indeed, the Spirit gave me the words to say, just as He promised.

What the Spirit Is Saying...

What did the Spirit surface in your life as you read this chapter? Have you been asking the right questions, or have you never considered that God has a purpose for your life? Did He personalize His constant activity in your life, inviting you to join Him? How have you responded to His activity? Take a moment in prayer.

Heavenly Father, I see now how deeply
You've been working in me all along.
Forgive my feeble response and open my
eyes and ears to see and hear You at work.
I do want to do Your will,
as you make Yourself known to me.
May my life be a channel for
You to bless those around me. Amen.

chapter five

OUR RESPONSE
TO THE GIFT

How we receive the gift of the Holy Spirit will determine the course of our life. Our response to the Spirit's work in our life is the reason we see Him working in power, or the reason we're frustrated in our walk with Christ. It's the determining factor in whether we'll experience the blessing of the Lord or His discipline.

The Holy Spirit desires full and complete control of our lives. Every ounce of our being must be fully surrendered to Him, so He can fully do the Father's will through us. The smallest part of our life not yielded to

Him may derail His work to accomplish the Father's will. This may be why the Bible employs such terms as being "filled with the Holy Spirit," and "baptism [meaning *total immersion*] of the Holy Spirit" to impress upon us how He must have complete control of our lives.

When we fully realize that God, through His Spirit, is actively at work in our lives, we ought to respond with a holy awe. There ought to come over us a trembling that we might upset the Holy Spirit. Paul said, "Work out your own salvation with fear and trembling; for it is God who works in you both to will and to do for His good pleasure" (Philippians 2:12–13).

Let's take a look at different responses to the Holy Spirit seen among people today.

GRIEVING THE SPIRIT

First, we can *grieve* the Holy Spirit: "And do not grieve the Holy Sprit of God, by whom you were sealed for the day of redemption. Let all bitterness, wrath, anger, clamor, and evil speaking be put away from you, with all malice" (Ephesians 4:30–31).

Simply put, sin in our life grieves the Holy Spirit. When we allow attitudes and actions to be controlled by the flesh instead of the Spirit, we offend the Spirit within us. When those actions cause a break in fellowship with another believer, it also causes a break in fellowship with Him.

The Spirit cannot lead us into God's blessing until we repent of our sin, so He immediately brings conviction of the truth and the strength to repent. Never forget that His work of confronting us with our sin is done from a deep sense of love. The initial response of the Holy Spirit to our sin is not anger. Our sin grieves Him, for He knows how it will rob us of God's best, and rob others of God's best through us.

RESISTING THE SPIRIT

Second, we can *resist* the Holy Spirit. Stephen told the people, "You stiff-necked and uncircumcised in heart and ears! You always resist the Holy Spirit; as your fathers did, so do you" (Acts 7:51). When our sin grieves the Holy Spirit, He immediately brings conviction. But when He comes to bring our sin to light, urging us to repent, we can resist Him. We can refuse to admit our sin, or soft-pedal its name so that it doesn't sound so bad. We call adultery an affair; homosexuality an alternate lifestyle; the murder of unborn babies pro-choice. We excuse our anger by blaming our past, we justify unforgiveness, and we refuse to heed the work of the Holy Spirit in our life. We resist His work to make us holy and acceptable to God, and become disqualified for service.

Perhaps the most common form of resistance is found in simple complacency. We aren't alert and looking for the Spirit's activity. We want His presence only when we call Him in to meet our needs. We resist Him in worship during the invitation when He brings conviction. We postpone the encounter for another time, never realizing that we're putting off God when we resist His Spirit. And when He speaks, we argue, offer another opinion, or tune Him out. But when He speaks, the issue isn't open for discussion; He's looking for immediate obedience.

One of the reasons we resist the work of the Holy Spirit is that He'll often speak through another person. We might not mind if He spoke to our hearts while we were alone with Him, but when He does it through another brother or sister in the Lord, we resist Him. A penetrating word in a sermon, a comment made in a Bible study group, or the private counsel of a friend can assault our pride, and we struggle. But Jesus said, "He who receives whomever I send receives Me; and he who receives Me receives Him who sent Me" (John 13:20). If we refuse to hear a corrective word from another Christian and separate ourselves from the life of God's people, we are not in a position to hear the Spirit. He works through other Christians, and we resist Him by not allowing them into our lives.

"It is an unspeakable holy and glorious thing that a man can be filled with the Spirit of God.
It demands inevitably that the present occupant and governor of the heart, our individual self, be cast out and everything be surrendered into the hands of the new inhabitant, the Spirit of God.
If only we could understand that the joy and power of being filled with the Spirit will come once we comply with the first and principal condition—namely, that He alone be acknowledged as our Life and our Leader."

—ANDREW MURRAY

The Spirit of Christ

QUENCHING THE SPIRIT

A third response is to *quench* the Spirit. Paul said, "Do not quench the Spirit. Do not despise prophecies. Test all things; hold fast what is good. Abstain from every form of evil" (1 Thessalonians 5:19–22). In this context, the quenching appears to involve hindering or stifling the Spirit in some way. When the fire of the Spirit is burning, someone pours water on it or turns a meeting away from the Lord by a selfish or carnal comment.

We often pray for revival or a great move of the Spirit, but are unreceptive when He comes. We wanted conviction among the lost, but He instead calls believers to repentance. We envision how the church will be blessed, but He takes the church in a direction we aren't comfortable with. Because the Spirit doesn't come as we want, we turn Him away. But if the Holy Spirit is truly God, we don't tell Him how to work in our lives—He comes with the right to do as He pleases.

All three of these attitudes—grieving, resisting, and quenching—will keep the Holy Spirit from working in and through our lives. Sadly, they're common in the church today. People don't want the Spirit of truth to reveal the truth about their lives. We even use Christian activity as a cloak to hide the truth from ourselves and others.

(from Henry) THERE ARE CONSEQUENCES

I was approached by a man once who confessed to me a tragic and disturbing testimony. Two years earlier, he'd been a pastor in a large church, but had become involved in an improper relationship with his secretary. He'd chosen to divorce his wife and marry the woman, shattering relationships with his family and friends. Now he was trying to get on with his life and find a place of ministry within the pastorate again. He looked to me and asked, "Would you pray for me?"

My response wasn't what he was expecting. In fact, he probably wanted to retract the request. I said, "Yes, I will pray for you, but you need to know how I will pray. I will pray that God deals with you in such a way, that anyone even thinking of doing what you've done will forever be deterred from such a grievous sin." That man had no idea what it meant to openly sin against God and the convicting work of the Holy Spirit. There are consequences!

One only needs to read Hebrews 10:26–29: "For if we sin willfully after we have received the knowledge of the truth, there no longer remains a sacrifice for sins, but a certain fearful expectation of judgment, and fiery indignation which will devour the adversaries. Anyone who has rejected Moses' law dies without mercy on the testimony of two or three witnesses. Of how much worse punishment, do you suppose, will he be thought worthy who has trampled the Son of God underfoot, counted the blood of the covenant by which he was sanctified a common thing, and insulted the Spirit of grace?"

ASSIGNMENT DEPENDS ON CHARACTER

We live in a generation that feels as though there should be no consequences to our sin—including no restrictions on our "spiritual gifts." We say to ourselves, "After all, God is love and He'll forgive. Can't I continue to serve according to my gifts?" It's true that He forgives the repentant sinner, but that isn't the issue. The assignments of God always depend on character, not "gifts." He'll bypass thousands of people with impressive "gifts" to find one person whose heart is pure.

The building of such character takes time. This is why it's important to respond when the Holy Spirit is working in your life. If you consistently resist the convicting work of the Spirit—who's trying to keep you from sin—you've just revealed a deep character flaw.

Remember, serving God is not a right, but a privilege. Never tell God what you think you ought to do; He doesn't care about that. He wants to work through you, but He chooses not to work through an unholy vessel that will not yield to His Spirit.

"God gives His Holy Spirit not to those
who long for Him, not to those who pray for Him,
not to those who desire to always be filled.
He gives His spirit to those who obey."
–HUDSON TAYLOR
Hudson Taylor's Spiritual Secret

FILLED WITH THE SPIRIT

The good news is that we are free in Christ not to quench or resist or grieve the Spirit. Every person has the ability, by creation, to walk in an intimate relationship with Holy God by being filled with the Spirit. Paul said, "Do not be drunk with wine, in which is dissipation; but be filled with the Spirit" (Ephesians 5:18). When we respond to His work and yield to His right to reign in us, He then fills us.

It's helpful to think of this filling in the context of the other three attitudes, for if we don't, we'll think of being filled with the Spirit as merely an additional blessing or an extra inheritance that other Christians don't have. It will cause us to strive after something beyond our grasp, and will cause much frustration.

The truth is this: If we aren't filled with the Spirit at any given moment, it's because of only one thing—sin. Through sin, we grieve the Spirit, resist Him, and quench His work in our lives. When our lives are clean, when we're walking in a right relationship with the Lord, the Holy Spirit has complete access to our lives.

From God's perspective, being filled with the Spirit is the normal Christian life, which is what He desires for each of His children. And the place of filling is at the cross, where Jesus forgives our sin and covers us with His righteousness. As we allow Him to remove our sin, He fills us with the Spirit.

The formula to living the Spirit-filled life is simple: Obedience. We have no need of the Holy Spirit if we aren't willing to do what God has asked of us. The power of the Spirit will be seen at our first step of obedience.

WHAT THE SPIRIT IS SAYING...

Has the Holy Spirit convicted you of any sin in your life, even while reading this book? Do not grieve Him any longer. Repent and turn from your sin and take hold of the promises of God. Allow the Holy Spirit to fill your life so that you can experience abundant life in Christ. Take a moment to pray:

Heavenly Father, I don't want to miss out on Your best.
If I've been grieving, resisting, or quenching
the blessed work of Your Spirit in my life,
then this is to my shame and Your dishonor.
May Your Holy Spirit search my heart and
see if there be any wicked way in me.
Forgive me, cleanse me,
and use me as You will. Amen

(In your prayer, you may want to name specific areas of your life you've been withholding from Him. Repentance must be specific.)

chapter six

THE ADVENTURE OF OBEDIENCE

When we allow Christ to function as Lord of our life and the Spirit is free to actively do His work in us, the difference will become obvious. Life no longer consists of merely doing good works for God. Instead, the Christian life proves to be an exciting adventure of walking in God's very presence.

(from Mel) TAKING THE PLUNGE

In my college days, I went with a group of friends to explore the beautiful Lynn Valley Canyon in North

Vancouver. In the valley was a fast-flowing river fed purely by snowmelt coming down off the mountains. At a certain point, the narrow white water briefly widened into a pool. A steep rock wall towered over the river as it guided the path of the water. As we approached, the girls gasped at the bravery of some men jumping off the cliffs. "They have no fear! I can't believe anyone would do that! They're so brave!" Well, as you can imagine, I was cool, willing to do whatever necessary to impress my friends. Before I had time to think about what came out of my mouth, I confidently announced, "I could do that!"

Immediately I realized that talk is cheap. Anyone can boast about things they haven't yet done. As I climbed up the "cliff of death," the people below looked smaller and the boulders beneath the crystal clear water appeared larger. I remember thinking, *Why did I open my big mouth?* There I stood at the edge of the cliff with nothing between me and a fifty-foot drop into ice-cold water. All I needed was the courage to do it.

I took one simple step and there was no turning back. The wind came rushing through my hair, and the adrenaline was surging. Fear turned to excitement. I plunged deep into the pool. Shooting out of the water to a crowd of cheering onlookers, my first thought was, *I am alive!* Second thought: *Let's do it again!*

THE LOOK OF ADVENTURE

Many believers are unwilling to take a step of faith and release their life into the Spirit's control. They remain comfortable within their range of talents, but hesitate to attempt anything beyond. But what an adventure it is to walk in the Spirit!

What does that adventure look like? What can you expect to experience when you choose to walk in the Spirit?

As you continue in this journey, you'll notice several distinctive characteristics of a person who has understood the Christian life and is walking in the Spirit.

SATISFACTION WITH CHRIST

First, there's *satisfaction with Christ.* This may sound simple, but it's absolutely necessary if we're to be of use to God. We must be satisfied in Him, or else we'll be constantly thinking of ourselves and our personal needs.

Jesus said, "Whoever drinks of the water that I shall give him will never thirst. But the water that I shall give him will become in him a fountain of water springing up into everlasting life" (John 4:14). A relationship with Christ satisfies, and the Holy Spirit is the key. Jesus also said, "If anyone thirsts, let him come to Me and drink. He who believes in Me, as the Scripture has said, out of his heart will flow rivers of living water." He satisfies! And John tells us that Jesus was speaking of "the Spirit, whom those believing in Him would receive" (John 7:37–39). The Spirit is the One who applies in our life all that Christ accomplished on our behalf.

"It costs much to obtain the power of the Spirit:
It costs self-surrender and humiliation and a
yielding up of our most precious things to God;
it costs the perseverance of long waiting,
and the faith of strong trust.
But when we are really in that power,
we shall find this difference,
that whereas before, it was hard for us
to do the easiest things, now it is easy for us
to do the hard things."

– A. J. GORDON

The Ministry of the Spirit

Once you recognize your need, Jesus says, "Come to Me and drink." Not to anyone else—not to a church, a ministry, or a noble cause—but *"Come to Me."* He gave His life that you might be filled. He laid aside His glory that you might be filled. He prayed that you might be filled. He ascended on high, sits on the throne, has all authority in heaven and on earth, and sent His Holy Spirit that you might be filled. He has prepared everything necessary to fill your life with rivers of living water that will refresh your soul, and He now extends the invitation: "Come and drink." And we're satisfied.

DISSATISFACTION WITH SELF

Satisfaction with Christ leads to *dissatisfaction with self,* another distinctive mark of those who walk in the Spirit. You'll discover that the Holy Spirit will always be urging you to put aside anything that will hinder your progress as your run the race set before you.

When we seek the Spirit, He will always seek to make us "holy and acceptable to God." One who is born again of the Spirit will be putting off sin and putting on righteousness (see Ephesians 4:17–24; Colossians 3:1–13).

You can easily tell a person who has come near the kingdom of God and is under the conviction of the Holy Spirit. That person's mouth is stopped—no more excuses, no more explaining away sinful behavior. He or she humbly kneels at the cross and says, "God forgive me, a sinner." That person's life is growing daily toward Christlikeness.

HUNGER TO KNOW CHRIST MORE

That leads to the next characteristic, a *hunger to know Christ more.* The words in the Bible about Christ are no longer hearsay, but He is real and personal in *your* life. The Spirit continually uncovers the riches of Christ, and you see Him as never before. And as your mind is occupied by thoughts of Christ, He occupies your life and actions as well, so that Christ is revealed in an ever-increasing measure.

Then we can say, as Paul did to the Christians in Philippi, "For to me, to live is Christ" (Philippians 1:21). And notice the intensity in Paul's voice as he later tells them, "I also count all things loss for the excellence of the knowledge of Christ Jesus my Lord…that I may know Him and the power of His resurrection, and the fellow-

ship of His sufferings, being conformed to His death"
(Philippians 3:8–10).

LOVE FOR GOD'S PEOPLE

Another characteristic of a person walking in the
Spirit—one that is especially obvious—is that they *love
the people of God*. They always seek to build up the body
of Christ and are willing to lay down their life for them.
The Spirit isn't given for the individual alone, but is given
to strengthen and build up the church (see Ephesians
4:7, 11–16).

One of the clearest evidences of a Spirit-filled life is
a person's interdependent relationship with the rest of
God's people. They love the family of God and are using
their gifts to strengthen and build them up. Paul said,
"We, being many, are one body in Christ, and individually members of one another" (Romans 12:5). It's never
a matter of finding your spiritual gifts and going off to
do your ministry alone or outside the context of the
church. Any equipping of the Spirit is to help bring every
member to complete Christlikeness.

One who is filled with the Spirit cannot stand outside the church and watch from a distance. It's spiritually

impossible! They realize that every Christian is a brother or sister in Christ. And in Christ, we are *blood relatives*. The words of John say it all: "By this we know love, because He laid down His life for us. And we also ought to lay down our lives for the brethren" (1 John 3:16).

WHAT THE SPIRIT IS SAYING...

After your first step of faith that brought salvation, have you continued to grow in your relationship to Christ through the Holy Spirit? Are you satisfied with Him, or do you find yourself in a "dry spell"? Is there clear evidence of the Spirit's work in your life? Are other people growing toward Christlikeness because of you? There's so much more to know and experience personally of God, so keep moving forward. Take a moment to pray:

Heavenly Father, keep my heart focused
on You and Your activity.
I want to experience You fully as I walk in the Spirit.
Show me what You're doing in my
life and in the lives of Your people
so I can make the adjustments necessary
to join You in Your activity.

I do want to please You and encourage
those around me.
Show me how I can practically be
a blessing and bring glory to You. Amen.

chapter seven

THE SURRENDER

The key to a growing relationship with God is to release your life to all of God and of His will that you know. Don't worry about the unknown; simply respond to what He has revealed. If you're faithful in a little, He will give you more. Don't just look toward some future time when He'll do great things in your life; each step along the journey is special.

You'll find also that your relationship to God is uniquely your own. He'll take you from where you are to where He wants you to be.

YIELDING TO THE SPIRIT'S WORK

You may have given your life to Christ, but have you understood that you must yield your life to the work of the Holy Spirit? There's no such thing as a "once-for-all" decision in the Christian life; it's a daily dying to self—daily seeking Him and bowing to His lordship. But that Spirit-led lifestyle must start somewhere. Have you made the deliberate decision to allow the Holy Spirit to have complete access to your life?

That question can be answered very easily by asking it another way: Do you make your decisions based upon your ability to achieve the results, or upon the Spirit's leading and equipping?

Don't determine your response to God by looking at your "gifts." Look at your Lord and say, "Yes, Lord! I know Your Spirit is present to enable me as I obey You. Thank You, Lord!"

(from Henry) THE ISSUE SETTLED

Many people have asked about the moment when I fully surrendered my life to the Lord. That moment occurred at the age of nine when I was confronted with a simple truth. God convinced me that He was God and I was not. It may sound simple, but that special encounter has shaped my life ever since, and I've never approached God any other way.

But it wasn't until my teen years that I began to understand the implications of this truth. At the age of seventeen, I was at a youth rally filled with people, but it seemed as though I were the only person in the room. God came to me and said, "I told you that I am God and have the right to your life. I am claiming that right tonight." In that call of God, everything came into focus as I understood what it meant to surrender my life. From that moment on, I settled the issue of Christ's lordship and have never turned back. I released my life as much as I knew as a teenage boy, knowing I would need the Holy Spirit to guide me. I set my heart to obey and have never had to go back through the process again. It was settled.

There's no need to wrestle with the decision to obey if He is Lord. I just need to know what He wants of my life. I've discovered over time that my response to each assignment determines what He will do next. And He has been everything He ever said He would be in my life.

(from Mel) RELEASING CONTROL

I became a Christian at age nine. It was a childlike faith, because that is all a child has! As I grew in my knowledge of the Lord, I realized God's call on my life. But it wasn't until some years later that I understood what that meant.

I was still trying to "do God's will" in my own strength and failing miserably. I was very active in church, a leader among my peers, and doing what I thought was best—but with no power. It was becoming obvious that I had no idea what to do; it was clear I was wasting time and missing God's purposes.

Thank God He got my attention! It happened through an accident I had on a temporary logging job in northern Canada. As I lay in the snow—my femur shattered from the impact of a fallen tree, my chain saw still buzzing, and the temperature at thirty-five degrees below zero—the Lord said, "If you're not going to be of any use to Me on earth, you have no reason to be here. I could take you home at any time."

In that moment I knew I had to give Him my entire life. It wasn't what I could do for God, it was what He wanted to do through me. And until that moment, I was scared to release control to Him. I finally realized that my body didn't belong to me; it was His to use as He wanted.

My life hasn't been the same since. That doesn't mean I've been coasting on cloud nine with miracles left and right, but that the Spirit has consistently taught me, shaped me, and used me for the Father's purpose. Each act of obedience has opened up new opportunities to serve Him.

SEEING THE SCARS

Anyone who yields his or her life to God will be greatly used by God to extend His great kingdom. The nature of God's great salvation is that you not only are brought into the family of God, but you're also given the privilege to be a part of His plan to redeem a world. He comes to every believer with the invitation to respond to His work in and around their life.

Does that get you excited? It ought to, for there's no higher calling in life than to have the God of the universe invite you to join Him. So stand ready to respond!

After Jesus was resurrected, a fascinating event occurred in the upper room when He appeared there to the disciples. He showed them the wounds on His hands and His side, as if to say, "Here is My identification...I am Jesus!" What a picture of love! Then He said to the disciples, "Peace to you! As the Father has sent Me, I also send you" (John 20:21).

This passage doesn't say what the disciples were thinking at this moment of their commissioning, but they must have been staring at those scars—scars that reminded them that there was a cost, there was pain, there was a cross for them to bear as well, for Jesus had just stated that they were being sent *just as the Father had sent Jesus,* to do the Father's will.

"Every element of our own self-reliance
must be put to death by the power of God.
The moment we recognize our complete weakness
and our dependence upon Him will be the very
moment that the Spirit of God will exhibit His power."

– OSWALD CHAMBERS

My Utmost for His Highest

Remember again, as we saw earlier, that when Jesus was sent by the Father, He was equipped with the Holy Spirit. In the same way, the disciples would be equipped with power from on high. Listen to the record of John immediately after this assignment was given to the disciples: "And when He had said this, He breathed on them, and said to them, 'Receive the Holy Spirit'" (John 20:22). Here was the enabling work of the Holy Spirit coming upon them.

Soon afterward, Pentecost was the moment when the Spirit was sent upon all believers in a permanent fashion. He came upon them to be Jesus in them, and much more. As Jesus taught, now the Spirit would teach. As Jesus comforted, now the Spirit would comfort. As Jesus led, now the Spirit would lead. Everything they would need would be found in Him who now dwelled within. And their mission would be the proclamation of the gospel of salvation throughout the world.

GOD WILL SHOW YOU

Listen to God's wonderful promise: "Thus says the LORD who made it, the LORD who formed it to establish it (the LORD is His name): 'Call to Me, and I will answer you, and show you great and mighty things, which you do not know'" (Jeremiah 33:2–3).

Are there things about God's will that you don't know? Then be ready for God to reveal His purposes through the Holy Spirit who dwells within you. Don't be in a hurry; simply trust that He'll show you in His time what's on His heart. He may cause you to wait before Him. He may choose to leave you in a difficult situation to see whether or not you'll remain faithful. He's far more concerned with who you are than He is with what you do for Him. So go to Him with an open Bible and ask Him to reveal His purposes for your life, purposes that were established before you were ever created.

The Bible teaches that nobody can thwart God's plans for you (see Jeremiah 32:17). Satan can't stop you, the world can't stop you, and circumstances can't stop you. "If God is for us, who can be against us?" (Romans 8:31).

(from Henry) COUNTING THE COST

I was leading a conference in Taiwan when scores of people began responding to the message on revival. Before I finished speaking, people began streaming forward.

When appropriate, I came alongside a young man who was kneeling at the front, for it was obvious the Holy Spirit was dealing with him. His eyes were swollen with tears and he was visibly shaking.

"It seems to me that God has spoken to you," I said.

He quietly answered, "Yes, sir."

"Do you mind telling me what He has said?"

He looked directly into my eyes. "God has told me I'm to go to mainland China and preach the gospel."

I asked if he realized this could cost him his life.

As he looked back at me, it seemed as though I could see right into his soul. After a moment he said through tears, "Sir—that is the issue I just settled with God a few minutes ago."

That young man had a profound encounter with God, and the Holy Spirit was guiding him in understanding it. The Lord was leading him to a new level of obedience that would be costly. But he surrendered his life to be used of God no matter what the cost.

Like Abraham climbing the mountain with Isaac to make the ultimate sacrifice, this man had a faith that was ready to say yes to anything God asked. And in the midst of tears, there was great joy that the Lord counted him worthy of such an assignment. But he didn't go alone; he went full of the Holy Spirit. His confidence wasn't in self, but in the Spirit's ability to work through his life to accomplish the Lord's will.

FREEDOM AS NEVER BEFORE

There comes a point in your life when the Lord opens your eyes to understand what the Christian life was meant to be. It isn't just going to heaven when you die; it's dying to self on earth and allowing Him to live through you.

Once that is clear in your heart, once you've chosen to release everything to Him, then you'll know freedom like never before. The burden of service dissipates and the Spirit will carry you into the Father's perfect will. And in that place you'll experience the mighty power of God. There are no more excuses for inactivity, no more justification for shallow character. There's only the Lord and our willingness to trust Him and respond to the Holy Spirit.

So the question comes to each of us: Who is the Holy Spirit to me? What have I done with Him? Or perhaps better said: What has He done with me?

Have you neglected God's gift of the Holy Spirit who has taken up residence in your life? Are you content to hear stories of great men and women of the past? Or do you want God to use your life?

If so, it's just a prayer away. This isn't a complicated

thing; just pray and ask God to fill you with His Spirit. As you've been reading, the Holy Spirit has been testifying to your spirit that you need to release your life to Him. Yield yourself as He begins to work in and through your life to accomplish the Father's will.

WHAT THE SPIRIT IS SAYING...

As you meditate upon the message you've heard in this book, has the Holy Spirit impressed upon you truth that requires a response? Is He moving you out of your comfort zone and into the Father's will? Scripture says, "Without faith it is impossible to please Him" (Hebrews 11:6). Are you doing anything that requires faith? Are you living in the power of the Holy Spirit, a power that is beyond your natural abilities? Perhaps you need to ask the Spirit to guide you in an appropriate response.

Father, thank You for the immeasurable
gift of Your Holy Spirit.
I now yield and surrender all of my life
to Him and to His working of Your
will in me and through me.
Thank You, Father, for hearing me

and immediately responding.
You are the Master and I am the servant.
Your servant is ready to obey.
Here I am, send me!

The publisher and author would love to hear your
comments about this book. *Please contact us at:*
www.bigchangemoments.com

WHAT HAPPENS
WHEN WE LISTEN TO HIM?

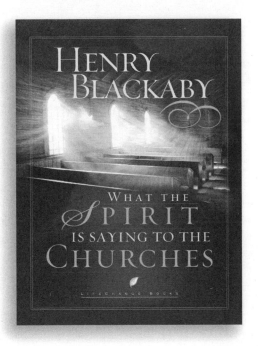

God has an urgent mission for you and your church to accomplish right
now. Noah built an ark. Moses confronted Pharaoh. Abraham went out,
not knowing where he was headed.... So what is He telling you? How
can you discover your unique assignment? Here's the record of one
church's pilgrimage from ten discouraged people on the verge of quitting
to a people who discovered their Lord and their calling.

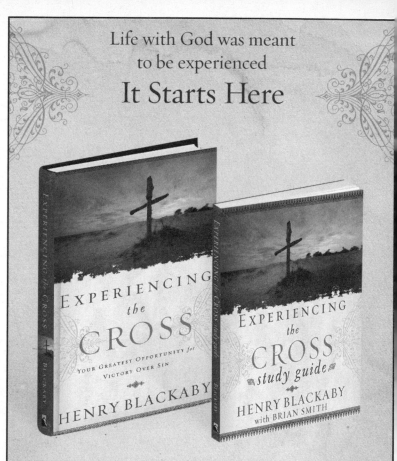

Life with God was meant
to be experienced

It Starts Here

Henry Blackaby leads you on an exploration through the deeper dimensions of the cross, ensuring that the further you go, the more you will: Deal radically and completely with sin, embrace true and lasting union with Christ, and experience the fullness and reality of His victory in your life. Will you yield to God's provision in His cross? Will you receive the power and presence of Jesus Christ? Will you dare to experience the cross?

Study Guide Also Available

Go Further With Your Experience

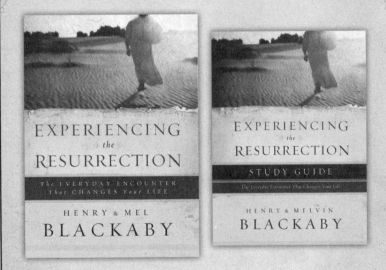

This book invites you to experience the living Christ in your life...day by day and moment by moment.

First you'll explore the meaning and purpose of the resurrection in the mind of God. Then you'll witness it in the life of the Lord Jesus. And finally you'll experience personally the peace, joy, power, authority, confidence, and hope the resurrection can generate in your life.

Study Guide Also Available

Let the Spirit Take You Beyond Yourself

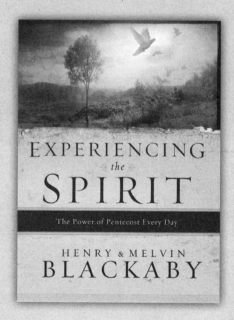

The first Christians "turned the world upside down" (Acts 17:6) shaking the gates of hell even in the face of severe persecution. The result: People all around "were filled with wonder and amazement" (Acts 3:10). What can give Christians today the same impact? God's Holy Spirit is ready to answer that for us in an awesome way, as Henry and Mel Blackaby make clear in *Experiencing the Spirit*. Release the Holy Spirit's work at the very core of your experience of the Christian life — as He releases you to serve God as never before.